MW01181034

FROM THE CRADLE TO THE MISSION FIELD: He Chose To Use The Most Unlikely Person

Copyright 2019 by Carolyn Routon

FROM THE CRADLE TO THE MISSION FIELD: He Chose To Use The Most Unlikely Person will take you on a journey through the life of Carolyn Routon. As the author shares her life with you in this book, you will see God's faithfulness demonstrated time and again. However, this book is more than just a history of the author's life. As you progress through this work, you will discover Biblical principles and lessons to learn and apply in your own life. This book should be read with a view in mind, and an openness to, what the Lord might want to accomplish in and through your life. More than a historical record, this book is intended to challenge you to be transparent in your prayer, fellowship, communion, and service to the Lord as you seek what His plans, purposes, and path are for your spiritual life journey. Read, digest, and absorb this book with an openness to how the Lord wants you to be used.

About the Author

Through the years, God has done more in and through me than I could ever imagine. There was a time in my life I didn't think God would ever use me again because of the choices I made and the sin in my life. I was sure those choices and sin once again drove the nails into the wrists of Jesus. Those thoughts entered my mind because I didn't really understand the depth of love which flows from His forgiveness. Jesus has put a love in my heart for evangelism, discipleship, and helping those who are hurting as a result of the choices they have made. I want to fulfill His Great Commission. God has allowed me to partner with Him to start two pregnancy centers in the state of Missouri, to serve among Native Americans in Oklahoma, and to minister as a missionary in the country of Haiti.

When in the United States, my husband Terry and I are blessed to stay in Warsaw, Missouri in a house which we were given. We have four children, ten grandchildren, and counting. We are blessed when we have time to spend with our precious grandchildren that all live within a three-hour drive of Warsaw, Missouri. We speak in churches and share individually about Haiti to increase awareness of the needs in that country, to gather support, and to encourage others to go on mission trips wherever God leads.

Acknowledgements

To my parents Elvin and Cornelia Fowler, who have left their earthly home for eternity in heaven. They chose to have a fourth child, when told they should not. They brought me up in the ways of the Lord.

To my brother. He helped lead me to make a decision for Christ at the age of 5 1/2. At that young age he guided me toward my need for Jesus Christ.

To my sisters. They always encourage and support me.

To my wonderful husband Terry. He loves and supports me in whatever God has called me, or us, to do.

And, last, to our children Myra, John, Mike, and Stefany. They have been through a lot over the years as Terry and I have followed Jesus, especially as we went to the mission field. Through it all they have understood. Our prayers for our children and grandchildren are that they will desire to follow Jesus as well.

Please feel free to connect, friend, or follow me on the following social media platforms:

Facebook:
www.facebook.com/carolyn.routon

LinkedIn:
www.linkedin.com/in/carolyn-routon-99345195/

Twitter:
www.twitter.com/carolynrouton

Blog:
www.routonshaitiblog.blogspot.com/

Email:
carolynrouton@yahoo.com

Endorsements

Greg Bunn, Pastor

I want to speak on behalf of the Haitian ministry of Terry and Carolyn Routon. This is not second-hand information because I have personally been to their area of ministry in the Northwestern Mountains on two different occasions. I have seen first-hand what they do, how the Haitian people respond to them, and how their ministry has grown.

Their personal testimony is what caused me to make the decision to travel to Haiti, which is one of the poorest countries, if not the poorest, on the planet. The Haitian people have had a difficult past, present, and future.

Spiritually leading the Haitian people are pastors with a heart for God, a love for the people, and a longing to be better preachers and pastors. These are pastors who want to be more equipped to fulfill their calling. Along with the spiritual needs are physical needs such as health care, medicine, food, and clothing. These people are dependent upon the weather to provide proper rain for their gardens, food for their animals, and food for the table. They are also dependent upon outside help when people of other countries decide to help.

My first trip to see the Routons in Haiti was really an awareness visit to provide education and encouragement for the Haitian pastors. I wanted to see what I could do. I led a pastor's conference where I learned what these men deal with in their churches and communities. I sensed their hunger for help, their frustration in dealing with false teachings, their concern for immorality in the community, and their concern for fellow pastors who were having relationship problems.

My second trip to Haiti included the same goals and same outcomes, but an additional focus was a conference for pastors and their wives as some were dealing with suffering relationships. This trip also included some one-on-one time with pastors as needed. I had heard the Routon's testimony and was interested in exactly what they were doing; as well as how the work was progressing. This is what I discovered.

1. They had intentionally made personal, close relationships with each pastor in their area. This was the key for the future of what they would be able to do.

2. They had been in each church, visited individually with each pastor as to how they could be of service, and had made relationships with the people.

3. They had started a weekly pastor's training/fellowship time each Friday, a sewing class for the wives, a children's program each Wednesday, a Vacation Bible School (VBS) in the summer, and avenues for helping families when in crisis. (Pastors would literally walk for hours to attend the weekly meetings as well as the daily conferences.) There is a booth at the weekly market for the purpose of giving water and having evangelistic conversations as opportunities come.

4. There were constant knocks at their door each day from people/pastors who needed to talk, people who needed help, and people who were passing by and just wanted to say "Hello."

5. Pastors were very open to talking to them about family problems, church problems, and struggles in dealing with the false teachings spread from people practicing voodoo, from other religious groups, from the long traditions of man, and from the larger churches that tried to put unbiblical principles/practices upon the smaller churches.

6. I saw the Routons functioning and practicing the ministries of what Directors of Missions might encounter.

Every day was a new day with new encounters and opportunities.

7. As a pastor, knowing the stresses of ministry, I saw them experiencing the same kinds of overwhelming stress, having the same constant concern for people, and doing everything with the resources they had to make provision in each situation. Like Jesus, there were times they needed to come apart before they came apart. They made sure there were times of refreshing so they could be ready for whatever came their way.

8. The Routons truly have a calling to this ministry. They have gone from one pastors' group to eight, some of which are hours away. They personally go to these groups to provide training and have trained local pastors to go and train others as well. They train leaders to be leaders.

9. Pastors are in contact with each other and keep the Routons informed of important needs. When the Routons are not in Haiti, some of the lead pastors take care of issues while they are away.

I would encourage anyone who can to make a personal trip to Haiti to see first-hand what ministries are in place there. You will be the one who will come away blessed as you seek to bless the Haitian people.

Alan Balmer, Author

My wife and I have known the Routons for over 8 years. In that time, we have seen their hearts, lives, and talents poured out for the lost and hurting through their ministry at the Door of Hope pregnancy center in Clinton, MO and through their missionary efforts in Haiti. Their receptivity and obedience to flow in the ways that God directs their ministry is much appreciated. We have seen them operate in multiple areas of ministry within their region in Haiti. Their discipleship and mentoring process, which is empowering the Haitian pastors, has resulted in a multiplication process that has been released in their region. Through the years of supporting the Routons, one of the conclusive, reflective, and provocative statements they have used in their emails is "Do you have your passport ready?" How can you be ready for missions outside your country if you are restricted to its borders as a result of the lack of a passport?

This book will help you see the spiritual fruit that can be achieved as a result of obedience to the moving of God's Spirit. I encourage you to challenge yourself as you read this book. Take time during the absorption of the material in this book to pray, then listen, then hear, and ultimately obey in that which you are being led.

Books by Alan Balmer

100 Day Vocabulary Word Devotional
http://amzn.com/B01NARVGW3

40 Day Lent Vocabulary Devotional
http://amzn.com/B01MYEKAP1

Tips and Advice To Get A Job And Advance Your Career
http://amzn.com/B06XK7DPZ6

Hiring By THE BOOK
http://amzn.com/1729409105

Contents

FROM THE CRADLE TO THE MISSION FIELD: He Chose To Use The Most Unlikely Person 1

Introduction: 15

Chapter 1: THE EARLY YEARS 17

Chapter 2: ENTRY INTO ADULTHOOD 21

Chapter 3: THE BEGINNING OF OUR FAITH JOURNEY 26

Chapter 4: MY FIRST HAITIAN STEPS... 28

Chapter 5: THE TRANSITION TO MORE 33

Chapter 6: TRUSTING GOD THROUGH THE TRIAL 37

Chapter 7: TIME TO TAKE THE LEAP.. 39

Chapter 8: THE ORPHANAGE YEARS IN HAITI 41

Chapter 9: A NEW WORK IN THE STATES....................................... 50

Chapter 10: ROUND TWO IN HAITI 54

Chapter 11: THE TEACHINGS... 64

Chapter 12: LESSONS WE HAVE LEARNED 67

Chapter 13: THE WOMEN OF HAITI 72

Chapter 14: A TYPICAL HAITIAN DAY 74

Chapter 15: WHAT WE HAVE LEARNED 79

Chapter 16: THE CALL TO ARMS.. 83

Chapter 17: A MISSIONARY... 93

Chapter 18: 20 YEARS AND COUNTING... 96

Chapter 19: THE WHY AND HOW.. 106

Chapter 20: CONCLUSION 111

Introduction:

Some may say where you grew up, what family you are a part of, and when you are born has no particular meaning for your future. But I say it does. **My parents were** told not to have any more children after their third child, my brother, was born. But God had another plan. Almost four years later, November 11th, 1956, I arrived. Had I been conceived twenty years later the doctors may ha**ve advised m**y mom to consider an abortion. There were probably times that my brother wished they had made him the last child. I was the youngest of four children, but my family was always very supportive of anything I wanted to do. I grew up on a farm. Many days during the summer I drank creek water. I learned to eat almost everything. With only a high school diploma, little did anyone know the plans God had for me until about 1994. Those plans were to help start two pregnancy center/maternity homes, go to the foreign mission field of Mexico, and the home mission field of Oklahoma to work with Native Americans. And, ultimately, to the foreign mission field of Haiti.

My mom told me once that I would make a good pastor's wife. She was close, as my husband Terry disciples pastors in Haiti. Terry was ordained as a pastor in Haiti. So, from the cradle to the mission field, God had a plan and He chose to use the most unlikely person.

Chapter 1: THE EARLY YEARS

God is so full of love, mercy, and grace that He never gives up on us. There is no greater place to be than in the will of God. As I share some of my childhood memories and the testimonies of what God has brought me through, you will see that to be true.

As a child, trips to North Carolina to see my maternal grandparents, aunts, uncles, and cousins were always the highlight of my summers. I learned quickly that grandma was a woman of God that prayed for us regularly. Her love for Jesus was greater than anyone I ever knew.   Another highlight of my childhood days was getting together with extended family regularly. I grew up with lots of cousins and we were all very close. Sometimes it seemed like we were related to everyone in the area. Warm remembrances include times when family and neighbors would come over and band together to help on projects like assisting my dad with farm duties or constructing a barn. Sometimes I miss those days.

Family devotions each night while growing up in Coal, Missouri are something I will always remember and treasure in my heart. Sometimes I remember falling asleep; especially during the prayer time. Going fishing, swimming in our pond, and playing ball with my family are all wonderful memories. One vivid recollection is when one of my sisters made her way to the center of the pond. After she had floated to the center of the pond, along with knowing that she didn't know how to swim, my dad had to go save her. After that dad thought it would be good for all of us to know how to swim.   So, he just threw me in the water and that allowed me to learn very quickly how to swim.

I asked Jesus into my heart at the age of five. I was water baptized very shortly thereafter in the pond of one of the local church members. Some may say that five years is too young to make a decision for Christ, but I knew I was saved. I remember the day I made a decision for Christ as if it were yesterday. I came to that decision for Christ one day when my brother asked me while we were playing if I was ready to ask Jesus into my heart. I said "Yes."

My sisters are nine and ten years older than me and at the young age of twelve I became an aunt. I thought it was awesome to become an aunt before any of my friends. At that young age, I had fun going to stay with my sisters for a few days. It allowed me to get away from my brother, but also to be able to play with my sister's babies.

I went to a one room schoolhouse for a couple years. That school was in Coal, Missouri. Later, another school was built in the same area. This was for the purpose of consolidating several one room schools into one bigger school, which grouped two grades per classroom. During my grade school years, the class sizes were small. Most of my fellow students attended church. At that age I thought if you and your family went to church, and you had a head knowledge about Jesus, you must be saved.

High school was a culture shock for this country girl. I carried my Bible to school every day in hopes that someone would ask me questions. I did not realize I was supposed to ask them if they knew about the Bible. I vowed to save sex until marriage. It was a difficult choice and my heart broke a few times while fulfilling that vow, but with the help of God's Spirit, which I knew very little about, I was successful in keeping that vow. Sadly, the Baptist denomination I grew up in didn't talk much about God's Spirit and the power I had within me. Or, if they did talk about God's Spirit, I didn't listen very well. However, my grandma helped me to begin understanding about

God's Spirit and that gave me a hunger to learn more. As I got out on my own, I began to do personal studies about God's Spirit.

Chapter 2: ENTRY INTO ADULTHOOD

Nine months after high school, at the age of 18, I married. This was another culture shock as I was very naive and did not really understand marriage. At the age of 23 I had my first child, a daughter. Then, three years later, I had a son. Two years later that marriage ended. Little did I know how satan works. Satan works most of the time when we least expect it. I was alone, scared, and sinking with two young children. My family tried to reach out, but I was ashamed. I knew I had disappointed and hurt my family and God. When the church did not reach out to me, I felt totally alone. As satan used the world to reach out to me, I swallowed the fake love bait hook, line, and sinker. I experienced the old saying, "jumping from the frying pan into the fire." My second marriage was worse than the first. When that second marriage ended, I sank to the bottom. Sometimes sinking to the bottom is what God uses to allow us to realize our need and total dependence on Him.

Finally, I allowed my family to reach out to me. Additionally, the church I attended at the time began reaching out to me. I was working a full-time job as well as serving in the local church and association (a group of local churches who work in conjunction with one another on projects.) The two children were my pride and joy. During this time, I knew I was saved, but something was missing. After two divorces, and being hurt by Christians as well as non-Christians, I began to pray, plead, and ask God to help. God led me to a book written by Kay Arthur titled, *Lord Heal My Hurts,* as well as His Word. As I read and studied *Lord Heal My Hurts,* along with the Bible, I began to see and understand how important it was to allow healing. I discovered that God does heal and forgive. As I continued in the healing process, I understood how to forgive those who had hurt me. The most difficult hurt, that took the longest to heal, was when my pastor at the time of my first divorce said, "I thought you were a saint. You can no longer serve in any capacity in the church." Another pastor helped in the healing process when he said, "God will use you again, just be willing and He will use you to help others."

In His timing, God showed up. However, His timing was not until I had been through two marriages and other failed relationships. I considered myself worthless and thought I was at the end of my rope. Then God showed up. As I got on my knees and cried out to Him, suddenly I felt like someone had wrapped their arms around me.

Softly I heard Him say, "I love you, I forgive you, and I will get you through this." I took my first actual step of faith that day and surrendered all to do whatever God asked me to do or go wherever He would lead.

Luke 9:23 became very real to me.

(NKJV) 23 *Then He said to them all, "If anyone desires to come after Me, let him deny himself, and take up his cross daily, and follow Me."*

I knew at an early age in life that I had experienced faith in Jesus Christ, by being saved by the grace of what He did while dying on the cross. However, I had not fully comprehended what it meant to be a follower of Jesus Christ because I had not been discipled; meaning to be taught about full surrender and abandonment to Christ. The process of being discipled started by spending much time in the Bible as well as at the feet and in the lap of Jesus. I searched for Bible study books that would help with topics where I felt I needed more information. Topics where I felt I needed more information were: God's Spirit, the fruit of the Spirit, who I was in Christ, and spiritual warfare. I stayed in church for worship, Bible study, accountability, and fellowship. I also began to see the importance of physical discipline and began an exercise routine. I want to encourage each of you reading this book that our physical well-being is an important complement to our spiritual health. Ultimately, this discipleship process resulted in the greatest joy, which was to embrace the principles in Luke 9:23 no matter the cost.

Even though I resisted the idea of another marriage due to trust issues, two failed marriages, abuse, and bad choices, God had another idea and brought a godly man into my life. God assured me that He had a plan and to just trust Him. I took another step of faith in 1994 when Terry and I were married. Terry had two beautiful children, whom I grew to love as my own. It was hard blending two families and there were times I know we would not have made it through without God being first in our lives; both separately and then as husband and wife.

Terry grew up in Sedalia, Missouri and at the age of 27 someone at his place of employment led him to accept Christ. *Experiencing God*, written by Henry Blackaby, was the first major Bible study we went through together in our church. The result was that we both truly experienced God. As we both totally surrendered to God, He began to work in our lives. At the time we did not know that surrender would mean serving Him in full time ministry. Additionally, we did not yet comprehend the full cost of abandonment to Him.

Chapter 3: THE BEGINNING OF OUR FAITH JOURNEY

One Sunday my pastor at New Hope Baptist Church in Sedalia, Missouri was preaching on what the Bible says about the value of unborn lives and being created in God's image. God's Spirit spoke to me on that day that I was to get involved in protecting the lives of the unborn. My life has never been the same. As I asked the church, friends, and family to pray, God began to show me to quit my job and trust Him to start a maternity home. I talked to Terry and he said, "If God has called you to do that, I will support you 100%." Initially, in 1995, this ministry started under the name, There is Hope. The first step in 1995 was a pregnancy center to help ladies choose life for their unborn children, as well as sharing the love and hope of Jesus Christ. At the time of the pregnancy center opening, the extended vision for There is Hope was to eventually provide housing for those that were removed from their residence. There is Hope accomplished the residential housing objective in 1997 and became a maternity home. The ministry of There is Hope was our first step of faith. That step of faith involved Terry financially supporting our household while I ministered to the community at There Is Hope. God honored that obedience. Eventually, God would ask Terry to transition from a full-time job to the ministry at There Is Hope. When that transition occurred, we functioned as house parents at There Is Hope. Each step of faith we took was bigger. As our faith grew, taking additional steps of faith became easier.

I encourage you to do whatever God's Spirit leads you to do. Taking those steps will be worth the cost because Jesus is worth it all. Whatever God calls each of us to do, if we will be obedient, He will make a way to equip us to do the work.

One fall evening in 1998 at our church in Sedalia, Missouri, a visiting pastor who had taken multiple missionary trips to Haiti came to give a presentation about Haiti. During the presentation, which included a combination of testimonies and pictures, God's Spirit said to me "Go." As I leaned over and shared with Terry what God's Spirit spoke, Terry said, "If God is calling you to go, I will support you, but I am never going to Haiti."   Those truly are "famous last words" and we have learned to never say "never."

Chapter 4: MY FIRST HAITIAN STEPS

In January 1999 I experienced the ultimate culture shock when I stepped off the plane in the foreign country of Haiti at the capital in Port Au Prince. No jet bridge (the tunnel that connects the plane to the airport terminal) existed. The combined smells and odors from trash, sewage, and dirty water running in the streets was overwhelming. I observed people urinating anywhere and everywhere, as there was no plumbing or electricity. Piles of trash were visible everywhere you turned. I was shocked by the sights, smells, and sounds experienced during this, my first ever trip to Haiti. This challenging entry into Haiti was in addition to the complications I experienced, in that the plane could not land on the originally scheduled day. On the previous day, the plane could not land due to electrical problems at the airport which caused total darkness. As a result, we had to fly to the next closest island to prepare for another attempt at landing in Haiti the next day. To say that these two events caused some concern for me regarding my introduction into Haitian culture is an understatement.

With those initial first trying days in the rear-view mirror, the mission team I traveled with began the ride up the mountains to our destination in the back of an old army truck full of people and supplies. Within the first few trips up the mountain, we quickly designated our "ride" up the mountains as "Six Flags Over Haiti." I quickly learned of the necessity to potty wherever we could find a bush big enough to hide behind. The drinking water was "treated" with purification tablets but sometimes either the treatment wasn't sufficient or the dust that was inhaled from "Six Flags Over Haiti" caused us to experience "Haitian happiness." We define "Haitian happiness" in similar terms to what in America we might call bathroom issues resulting in both ends being adversely affected.

Upon arriving at the Haitian village, I slept in a hut with a thatch roof and dirt floor. Critters fell from the roof and landed on me while I was asleep. I saw little babies, toddlers, and some adults experiencing starvation. It was overwhelming to experience the number of people asking for a piece of bread or a dollar. I experienced sadness, tears, and compassion for the Haitian people who had medical problems for which I could not provide assistance. I saw more poverty than I believed could ever exist in our 21st century and felt helpless as I thought there were more needs than could ever be met. I was shocked to learn that if ladies didn't wear skirts or dresses, they would be thought of as a prostitute. All women wore a customary head covering.

Despite all these difficult observations, experiences, and emotions, I quickly learned to listen to God's Spirit allowing Him to show me what to do and how to help. Additionally, I learned to appreciate the Haitian people's hard work which only resulted in just enough to survive. Furthermore, and probably most important, I grew to long for the same joy exhibited during their style of worship, sensing that, despite being physically poor, they were spiritually rich.

During this two-week time in Haiti, which was my first ever foreign mission trip, I experienced God moving in ways I had not experienced before. I had only taken enough supplies to conduct a Vacation Bible School (VBS) for 300 children as that was the number of children for which I was asked to prepare. All 300 children were in one building with only me and an interpreter. That was very challenging. During this trip, a pastor from another village asked me to come and share Jesus with the children in his church. I prayed about the request, telling God that I didn't have enough supplies for a second VBS. However, I also told God and the pastor that I would go when the first VBS was finished. When I went to do the second VBS, I unloaded the supplies. To my surprise there were exactly enough supplies needed for the additional 100 children who were present. This experience caused me to reflect on the Biblical account of five loaves and two fish where God's faithfulness to provide was displayed. This miracle caused me to grow my faith through experiencing a similar provision to that which the disciples' witnessed. The Bible account of multiplication came to life in me that day as it was no longer just a "story", but a real-life experience.

From 2000 to 2003, I continued to take several two-week trips to small villages in Haiti to help conduct VBS as well as to assist with medical mission teams. On one of those trips, during a four-hour ride to a medical clinic, I held in my arms a two-year-old toddler who had AIDS. I cried all the way back when we had to deliver the news to the toddler's family that there was nothing the clinic could do for her. I never did hear what happened to that child, but the experience impacted me profoundly. God spoke to me each trip that He was not finished with me in Haiti. Additionally, I came to understand that God had more for Terry and me than just two-week trips.

Those short-term mission trips to Haiti impacted my life in ways that are hard to describe. God used each trip to burden my heart more and more to serve in Haiti and, ultimately, to go and make disciples.

Chapter 5: THE TRANSITION TO MORE

Every time I went to Haiti, I felt more compelled that God was calling me to do more. But Terry was still not willing. On a trip to Haiti in 2000, I came back and asked my three prayer partners to join me in prayer for Terry regarding his role in Haiti. I also asked God to keep my mouth sealed so that I would not say anything, but only pray. Then I asked God for a confirmation that He was working in this matter.

Terry began talking about downsizing by selling our house and buying a smaller one. I was not on board with Terry's plan because of Haiti, but I went along for the ride. One day, as we were out driving looking at smaller houses, suddenly Terry said, "one day we may be living in Haiti." I asked Terry, "Why did you say that?" Terry responded, "I know that is in your heart." I knew that was my confirmation. I then told Terry the rest of the story. After that discussion, Terry quit looking to downsize and instead started seeking the Lord about Haiti. Not long after, Terry surrendered to God's Spirit to go to Haiti. As the time approached for this 2001 trip, I backed out of going on the trip with Terry as I sensed that God needed Terry to be alone on this trip so He could reveal things privately to Terry. After Terry came back from that trip, all he could say over and over was, "I am hooked on Haiti." Oh, the power of prayer!

The miraculous experiences witnessed by Terry while on this trip to Haiti are what I believe to be the reason he was hooked on Haiti. Prior to leaving for this trip, Terry had a friend come to the house. The friend took a bandana, anointed it with oil, and prayed over the bandana as well as over Terry. After the prayer, the friend instructed Terry to take the bandana to Haiti. The friend encouraged Terry that if anyone was sick to lay the bandana over them while praying and reading Scripture. The Scripture Terry used in his prayers for the sick was James 5:13-16.

> **(NKJV)** 13 *Is anyone among you suffering? Let him pray. Is anyone cheerful? Let him sing psalms. 14 Is anyone among you sick? Let him call for the elders of the church, and let them pray over him, anointing him with oil in the name of the Lord. 15 And the prayer of faith will save the sick, and the Lord will raise him up. And if he has committed sins, he will be forgiven. 16 Confess your trespasses to one another, and pray for one another, that you may be healed. The effective, fervent prayer of a righteous man avails much.*

On this short two-week trip to Haiti, one of the main objectives was to build a church. Unfortunately, after Terry and the rest of the team took the "Six Flags Over Haiti" ride, some of the team members experienced "Haitian Happiness" which could have caused the church building project to go unfinished by the end of the trip. Terry and those unaffected by "Haitian Happiness" took the anointed bandana and prayed over the team. Miraculously, the typical three days of "Haitian Happiness" were not experienced and the crew started back on the building project the next morning. The church building project was, in fact, completed prior to the end of Terry's trip.

During this trip, another powerful experience for Terry was when he went to a school for the purpose of sharing the gospel and distributing small toys to the children. After sharing the gospel and inviting the children to pray with him, 11 of the 22 children accepted Jesus Christ as their Lord and Savior. Terry said having those children accept Christ, on his birthday, resulted in the best birthday he had ever celebrated.

After Terry returned from Haiti, we began seeking the Lord regarding our next steps. We eventually sold our home and took the position of house parents at There is Hope. We did not know that our time at the maternity home would help prepare us for Haiti. In the fall of 2002, at a Mission Celebration with our association of churches, we committed our lives to full time mission work and believed the field to be Haiti.

Chapter 6: TRUSTING GOD THROUGH THE TRIAL

Just a few months after we made the commitment in the fall of 2002, satan attacked me with breast cancer. I had just previously had a mammogram with no sign of a lump or any issue. The lump just appeared, and we believed it to be a direct attack to get us off God's plan. We held on to the promises from God's Word and believed the call He had put on our lives. We trusted that He would heal me. I had a lumpectomy and radiation. The night I got home from the hospital, and was supposed to start radiation in a few days, I told Terry to go on to church without me. As he left, I began to cry uncontrollably. I turned on the radio, which was set to Christian music, and the radio announcer shared a Scripture, Joshua 1:9. It was as if that verse was shouting at me. After the verse was shared, I continued to cry more, but I had a peace that I cannot explain. Ever since that experience, Joshua 1:9 has been my hallmark verse.

> *(NKJV) 9 Have I not commanded you? Be strong and of good courage; do not be afraid, nor be dismayed, for the Lord your God is with you wherever you go.*

My surgeon encouraged us not to go to Haiti. After he saw we were committed he said, "I wish I had your faith." We were left with a $10,000 medical bill but otherwise had no debt. As we began to make plans to go to an orphanage in northwest Haiti in January 2004, some of our family questioned, "Why?" Others told us we were crazy. Our response to all was that we must be obedient to God's call no matter the cost. Obedience is greater than sacrifice. Terry had already quit his job, so we had no income. The hospital said we could pay fifty dollars a month. We sensed that God would provide and ever since that moment He has provided. We both agreed we would not let satan, anyone, or anything else steal our joy. We pressed on. God is the Great Physician and I have been cancer free since 2003!

Chapter 7: TIME TO TAKE THE LEAP

Our trip to Haiti in 2003 was for the purpose of settling our plans regarding where we would minister upon our return in January 2004. As we got to Haiti, we met a girl who had breast cancer and needed help financially for her surgery. God revealed to me, that if I would help the girl, He would take care of us and our bill at the hospital. I prayed. The next morning Terry came to me and said, "You want to help that girl with breast cancer, don't you?" I said "Yes, how did you know?" God's Spirit had told him. We didn't have much income, but we gave what we had to the girl. It was enough to assist her with breast cancer treatment. I did not tell Terry, or anyone else, about what God said to me regarding our personal hospital bill. A couple years later, while on the Haitian mission field, my mom wrote me a letter and explained that the hospital heard about the missions work we were doing in Haiti. As a result of that Haitian mission work, the hospital decided to release us of the now $9,000 debt. I then shared with Terry what God told me years before about His provision in response to our faithfulness with the girl who had breast cancer. We both rejoiced with tears of joy.

Upon returning from our 2003 trip to Haiti, we spent the next few months raising support. We never took our eyes off Jesus nor that to which He had called us. We are not what is thought of as your normal denominationally based missionaries. Our home church has always provided accountability for us as we are not a part of a mission's board or organization. We raise our own support from churches and individuals. We sold our home and all our possessions and went to Haiti by faith, totally on our own, not exactly sure what we would be doing.

Chapter 8: THE ORPHANAGE YEARS IN HAITI

In January 2004 we left the comforts of America and went to be mom and dad to twenty girls in a very remote part of northwest Haiti. We had no electricity, no plumbing, no vehicle, and very little money. But oh, the joy we had in serving our Lord! Focusing on what Jesus did on the cross was what brought us through.

The first six months of 2004 were very hard. However, God knew just what we needed, and He made provision. We walked to get water, food, and internet connectivity in order to communicate with family. We even went on walks to see other remote parts of Northwest Haiti. We walked everywhere because we did not have any transportation. That first month we had to walk over a mile from a guest house to the orphanage while we worked on the three rooms where we would live. We lived in the same house with the girls. The following paragraphs will outline some of the 2004 experiences during our initial six month stay in Haiti.

The spiders, roaches, and rats were larger than we ever imagined. One time I was in our outside toilet and a huge spider got between me and the exit door. I yelled for

Terry, but he didn't hear me. I was finally able to get the door open and it spooked the spider to the outside wall. Suddenly, a chicken saw the spider, dove for him, and ate the spider. After that I was tempted to have a chicken for a pet in the house, but due to the messes chickens make, we decided it was not a good idea.

One morning in Haiti I got up and felt prompted by God's Spirit to make some no bake cookies. I hesitated a bit, but the prompting became stronger, so I decided to make the cookies. That afternoon, an American who was in the area stopped by. The American was in our area handing out Gideon bibles. We had no idea he was in our area until he knocked on the orphanage door. He had been in the northwest Haiti area for a couple of weeks. We invited him in and visited for a while. While we were visiting, I asked him if he would like a drink or a cookie because I didn't have any other food to eat. He looked at me and said, "You may not believe me, but when I got up this morning, I just asked God if I could have a cookie." I thought, wow, God even answers prayer requests for small things.

During this six-month trip we went to another village to be involved in a house church service. I was standing on the road, inviting people to come into the service. One lady said, "No, I don't have a head covering to wear." I had a scarf on my head because I didn't want to draw attention to myself or offend anyone. I immediately took my scarf off and put it in my pocket in order for her to feel more comfortable to attend the service. Reluctantly, she came into the service. At the end of the service, she accepted Christ as her Lord and Savior. I began to realize that some of the Haitian customs prevent people from coming to Christ.

One morning I went for a walk and felt prompted by God's Spirit to go down a certain path. As I reached the end of the path, someone yelled "Madam Terry", which is what Haitians call me. I walked over to him and realized his housing situation was in great need. He told me his home had flooded a couple of nights prior when it rained. I realized he had started building a new house but did not have the means with which to finish. I walked away in tears, crying out to God regarding how we could help this family. I was prompted immediately by God's Spirit to send out an email to our prayer partners and those who financially support us, in order to state this family's need. I sensed that God would take care of the rest. I sent the email with the need for $2,000 to finish the family's house.

The next day I received an email stating that the check was in the mail.

One of our more frightening encounters was when some of the girls at the orphanage came running to our door and informed us that there was a man with a gun in the yard asking for us. We did not go outside and waited for the Lord to handle this situation on our behalf. Soon the girls came back to let us know that the villagers who were close by came and instructed the man to leave us alone as we were there helping the community. The man left and never returned. We praised the Lord as we experienced the Lord as our Protector.

The next story Terry calls, "the night of the attacking spider." I had gone to bed and Terry stayed up to read some notes he had in a notebook. Suddenly, he saw a huge spider on the floor looking straight at him. The next thing Terry knew the spider was coming straight at him. As the spider got to Terry's feet, Terry decided to throw the notebook on the spider to squash it.

We had a tin roof with gaps in the roof, so the rats were always running on the rafters. We were able to find some rat poison. Then the rats started dying right on the rafters. They would lay there until they would fall off.

As we arrived in Haiti in January 2004, the president of Haiti was ousted. We were warned by everyone to leave because no one knew when planes would be able to come and go in Haiti again. We knew God had brought us there for such a time as this, so we took another step of faith and stayed in Haiti despite the warnings. Our supplies got stuck in Port au Prince because of that situation.

A couple months passed, and we had no supplies while our money was running out. One day we looked to get something out of the one piece of luggage we had, and there we found 170 dollars laying in the suitcase. We had been in that bag many times before and never saw the money. That 170 dollars was just enough to get us through. The next month our supplies came with only one barrel missing. Some had told us we would never see any of our items again. We were told by the driver that they hid in the mountains until it was safe to pass with our possessions. God is good all the time, and all the time God is good!

The girls in the orphanage were in rags when we arrived in 2004. We had no outhouse, only a hole in the ground. Making changes took time and money but we finally got some clothes for the girls and an outhouse with a seat and roof. Spiders, roaches, rats, dust, and sickness were, at times, enough to make us want to quit. God wouldn't let us quit. He got us through that first year by ending it with shouts of joy. Those shouts of joy came primarily as a result of God's healing power as well as nine girls giving their lives to Jesus Christ. We went back to the states in June 2004 and then returned to Haiti in August 2004. We did not go back to the states for Christmas 2004. It was hard not being with family that Christmas, but God had other plans.

Even though we could not speak the creole language very well yet, we loved the girls and did what we could to share Jesus with them. God's Spirit did the rest. We were encouraged by the nine girls who accepted Jesus during our Christmas devotions. Ephesians 3:20 became very real to us.

> *(NKJV)* 20 *Now to Him who is able to do exceedingly abundantly above all that we ask or think, according to the power that works in us,* 21 *to Him be glory in the church by Christ Jesus to all generations, forever and ever. Amen.*

We should have had an interpreter with us to help, but because of the problems in Port Au Prince, the interpreter was not able to get to us. The girls were great to assist in helping us learn the language. I remember the excitement in my heart the first time I understood someone talking to me in the Haitian language. We have never mastered the language, so when we disciple or evangelize, we do use interpreters to make sure the Haitians understand.

One evening one of the girls, a four-year old named Love, was crying. The girls and their nanny came to get me. We prayed and sang as there was not much medical support available, especially that time of night. Love kept saying she hurt. We all went to bed not knowing what to expect, realizing it was up to God. The next morning, the girls came running to get me. They knocked on the door and Love was standing there. She said "Mama", which is what they called me, "I don't hurt anymore." I picked her up and we began crying and praising God!

Some of the girls did not know how to read their own language, so Terry and I worked with them every day on reading or math. A Haitian man from the village came to the orphanage while a mission team from the states was there to help. He heard us talk about Jesus and then left.

He came back a few weeks later and said he wanted to know more about this Jesus we serve. He knew some English and we knew some creole. We showed him scripture in the creole translation. He received Christ that day.

One day God's Spirit revealed to us that the Haitian man that owned the orphanage was not doing things in a righteous manner. We confronted him but to no avail. God said "Go." We put the girls with families and proceeded to help them learn a sewing trade. After the girls finished sewing school, we were able to present them with a treadle sewing machine which our supporters helped purchase. We experienced tears of joy the day we presented the sewing machines to the girls. They were so thankful that God had sent someone to show and share the love of Jesus through the avenue of providing sewing machines. During these times the girls in the orphanage learned to know God and were very thankful. We still keep in contact with most of the girls that live in our area.

As time went on, God led us to start a church in the village called MareRouge. Soon after the prompting of God's Spirit, and before we approached anyone about starting the church, the man that previously came to know Jesus approached us and said, "I feel led to start a church at my school. Will you help me?" That was confirmation to Terry and me that God was on the move and we needed to join God in the journey. In this new church plant, people came to know Christ. As a result, some felt impressed to start churches in other villages. The man who initially got saved, and was now pastoring the church, asked us if we would help him go to seminary. The seminary is located in the north, near Cap Haitian.

The experiences in our initial orphanage years were not all positive. We suffered physical sickness, language barriers, threats against us, as well as doubting if we belonged in Haiti. Another difficult part was missing our family. Our children were beginning to marry, and we expected grandchildren would be on the way. However, at the end of this time in Haiti, we looked back at the positive experiences and stories we have outlined in this chapter and realized that God did have a purpose for us in Haiti. We returned to the United States with a new optimistic outlook for our future efforts in Haiti. We felt God saying that the battle belonged to Him, and that He would direct our timing to return to Haiti.

Chapter 9: A NEW WORK IN THE STATES

We continued to make yearly trips back to Haiti in order to check on the church and sewing school. We continued serving the Lord in different ways. God sent us to Mexico on a mission trip with our church. While in Mexico for a week, we helped build a house and shared the love of Jesus. God spoke to us in Mexico that He was not done with us in Haiti yet, and to be patient while continuing to listen and follow His leading. Then, in 2008, we went to Oklahoma to help Native Americans. We were in Oklahoma for three months to work with the Native Americans among five different churches. We helped one church get their children's ministry revitalized by going door to door, as well as helping with Vacation Bible schools. We also helped put a new roof on the church building. We attended two different camp meetings. The first camp meeting we participated by teaching the youth for a week. During the second camp meeting we went to be participants. God spoke to me at that second camp meeting. When we arrived at the meeting, there were a total of six people in the sanctuary as the praise and worship service began. The lady that was leading worship pointed to me and said, "Come forward, I have a word from the Lord for you." As I approached the front she continued, "You will be ministering to a lot of women soon." I began to cry because I had asked God to speak to me at this meeting. I knew this message was what God was speaking as confirmation to start another pregnancy center.

While we were in Oklahoma, we received a couple of calls to go to Iowa and help start a pregnancy center. After talking with the individuals from Iowa, God said "No." Then God began to put in my heart to go back to my hometown of Clinton, Missouri and start a pregnancy center. I also felt that would be followed later by starting a maternity home. At first, I argued with God saying, "Why there? I have been gone a long time." Then, during that camp meeting and through the message that came from the lady that called me up front during the worship time, I cried and said, "OK God. I will go." So, again, we took a step of faith.

After the summer was over, God said "Go." We went to Clinton, Missouri seeking God for answers. God was already working. One of the first people I talked to suggested that I speak with another lady in town as she had similar thoughts about the ministry I was interested in starting. I contacted this individual and we began the mission God put before us. Another lady told me she had been praying for several years that God would bring someone to Clinton, Missouri to start a pregnancy center.

The church we helped start in Haiti gave us a love offering when we left and said to use it as seed to start whatever God called us to do. We put the $75 they gave us in the bank and it quickly grew to $10,000. In May 2009, the Golden Valley Door of Hope (pregnancy resource center) opened its doors in Clinton, Missouri. A couple years later a man walked in my door at the pregnancy center. He said he had been at the Door of Hope banquet fundraiser and God's Spirit had revealed to him that he needed to come volunteer at the Door of Hope. When the man walked in and sat down with me at the Door of Hope, God's Spirit told me, "He is your replacement. Train him and get ready to go back to Haiti." I did not want to scare him off, so I did not tell him that just yet. Over the next year we worked toward that transition goal, and in January 2013 Terry and I took another step of faith and returned to Haiti. Again, it was hard leaving family, especially with five grandchildren at that time.

Our time in the United States from 2008-2012 was bittersweet. We enjoyed spending time with our grandchildren; at that time we had three. Our parents were getting older so it was good to spend some final time with them, as we did not know when God would take them home. The other side of the coin was that we previously had a hard time leaving the Haitian brothers and sisters we had come to love and wanted to return to them.

Chapter 10: ROUND TWO IN HAITI

After four years (2008 - 2012) of helping a new church start in the village of MareRouge, making regular trips to Haiti, and spending a month each time with them, we felt the nudging of God's Spirit. That nudging was to expand to not just helping one pastor but discipling many pastors in the area. We began to realize the need for discipling as we spent time with other pastors. Most pastors in the area where we minister in Haiti do not have the possibility to get more training.

This new season of our lives, beginning in 2013, had God continuing to enlarge our territory. He always made a way and equipped us for the work. We taught the basics to see where the pastors were spiritually. Many pastors left the group because we told them we were not there to help build buildings and provide things but, rather, to disciple them in order to evangelize, disciple, and continue the cycle of evangelism and discipleship. We saw the need to build unity, so that is where we started.

We invited approximately 60 pastors from our village and surrounding area to come to our home for an initial meeting. We ended up meeting in our front yard because so many came. Over the next few weeks that group of 60 pastors shrunk to 35. Some left because they were not seeking God but, rather, seeking what they could extract from Terry and I, as Americans. The remaining 35 pastors became excited as they learned why God had called Terry and me there. That purpose was for discipling and equipping. After about a year had passed, one of the pastors asked us to help him start a group in his area. Then, as a few more months passed, more new pastors came asking us to start discipleship groups in their areas. The pastors began to share with other pastor friends, and over the course of the next four years the groups grew to thirteen, which totaled over 200 pastors. We believe the number of groups will continue to grow. The spark that began in our front yard is spreading, and we believe God is up to something. He is on the move in Haiti.

When we began meeting regularly with pastors, God prompted us to keep attendance. We believe that attendance shows us who is committed. Out of that original group of 35 pastors, God prompted us to choose a group who had been faithful in attendance. When we were finished choosing, there were 12 men in the group. We call this our gold group. After about a year we realized why God had us select 12 men for the gold group.

Ultimately, it became apparent and important to take our gold group of 12 pastors, divide them into six groups of two, and release them to begin discipleship groups in other villages. This began a process of spiritual multiplication by the local Haitian pastors that Terry and I could have never accomplished on our own. The process of choosing and discipling this gold group, to the point they were ready to go out, was about 3 years. 12 disciples, 3 years, sending out 2 by 2. Does that sound familiar?

The impact of this "sending out" process was that the teaching materials which we supplied and sent with our gold group were discovered by other area pastors with whom we did not have previous contact. One of those pastors inquired from where the teaching came. After being given the answer, that pastor asked Terry and me to help him start a group in his area. As this pastor stated, "We don't have that kind of teaching available."

Our long-time translator came to us and said he had learned much and felt called to be a pastor. He started a church in his home. He wanted to teach the truth that he had been taught, as opposed to the false teachings of the culture and other churches. That church doubled in the first year.

After our translator became a pastor, he met a man at a local store. The store owner told the pastor not to talk to the man because the man was a mean drunk. Our translator, the new pastor, spoke to the man. The man spoke back and said, "I am not the man they say I am anymore. God is doing something in me." The pastor told the man about Jesus, invited him to church, and offered to give him his shoes. The man thanked him and said, "I have been looking for someone like you to talk to me about Jesus and provide help." The man came to church and got saved the next Sunday. He also brought six people with him, two of which were his brothers.

It has been exciting to watch the discipleship process yield increased numbers for the Kingdom. The spiritual growth, as well as increased knowledge of the Lord and the Bible has been tremendous. Because the illiteracy rate among the Haitians church members is so high, the people will only grow as much as the pastors know. In Haiti, help is much more accepted when it comes from those pastors who have been set free from their own culture. One time Terry went with the pastors to minister. As the group approached one man, they shared the gospel with him. That man accepted Christ's invitation to follow Him and then said, "I have been waiting for someone to tell me about Jesus." This story really spoke to us about always being ready, as you never know when someone is waiting as God's Spirit is working in their life.

As Terry discipled the pastors, I also discipled the wives and some other ladies from the church. I didn't want to turn anyone away who wanted to know about God's Word. Someone in the ladies group told me that one of the other ladies who was attending was not married but living with a man. As I prayed, God's Spirit led me to some scriptures which I could share with her. One afternoon after the discipleship class, I asked her to stay. As I shared with her the truth from God's Word, I began to see tears in her eyes. I asked her why she was crying. She said that no one had shared with her what the Bible said on that matter. Furthermore, she could not read and therefore could not discover on her own. She and the man decided to live in separate houses until they could arrange to be married. A sad point to this account is that she has three brothers who are pastors. Instead of them guiding her through Biblical principles, they just abandoned her.

A cultural issue in Haiti is the prevalent thought process that says you must have a lot of money to have a wedding, a ring, a big celebration, the right clothes, and a properly equipped house. Again, I shared with her from God's Word showing her that those cultural thoughts are not in the Bible. The snare from satan is that if you don't have the money, you just live together. That couple got married in our front yard in Haiti. The pastors that Terry disciples came to perform the ceremony. It was a simple wedding. Both husband and wife were excited. In the weeks ahead, she would come to the ladies' study class with a joy on her face that cannot be described. She began to share with the group how God was blessing them in ways they had never seen. They both believed the blessings were because of their obedience to God and His Word.

We also trained some of the local teachers to go into the schools with the gospel as well as a message of sexual purity until marriage. In Haiti, the gospel message can be shared in the public schools. We have had some students ask for more information about the gospel as they had never heard the gospel message. Some students received Jesus Christ as a result of those efforts.

Another effective method of sharing the gospel has been in the local markets. We helped pastors set up booths in their local markets. The booths are for a dual purpose: giving away water and sharing the message of Jesus Christ.

Through these efforts many have gotten saved or have recommitted their lives to Christ.

We are helping pastors start small businesses by loaning them 200 US dollars to be paid back over a 27-month period. This helps the pastors to support their families as many don't receive a salary from the church they serve. When the pastors pay back the loan amount, we are able to take those funds and assist another pastor with that initial seed money of $200. This is a growing part of our ministry which we look to develop further as God makes a way through our prayer and support team members. We believe that our example of small business assistance loans with local pastors will have a trickle-down effect, inspiring this model to be used for the benefit of church family members needing assistance in their personal endeavors for creating small businesses.

Many people have come from different countries, including the United States, with a handout which has caused a lot of problems for the Haitian people. It has also caused problems for the full-time missionaries who live among the Haitians. The Haitians see missionaries and automatically think and say, "What are you going to give me or do for me?" Many in the older generation still have pride and want to find ways to provide for their family. But, many of the younger generation think they are entitled and want others to come and meet their needs. It has created a dependency model. If you want to know more about the pitfalls of a hand-out as opposed to a hand-up mentality, a couple of good books to help you fully understand are *Toxic Charity* and *When Helping Hurts*.

The vision we have for the ministry is called:

Psalms 133 Haiti Ministry

Psalms 133 Haiti ministry is to build unity among pastors and is based on Psalm 133:1.

(NKJV) 1 Behold, how good and how pleasant it is

For brethren to dwell together in unity!

Unity is achieved by building groups that meet regularly for the purpose of sharing the Word, equipping the pastors with the truth, and providing teachable biblical lessons in their language. This has all been established in order to rid the pastors from the influence of voodoo, false teachings, and the traditions of man that are in opposition to the Word of God.

As missionaries, we always look forward to seeing how God works through the lives of those we disciple. As we see God moving and working through the pastor's willing hearts, we are like proud parents watching their children walk across the stage to receive a diploma.

One thing we discovered through the process of trips back to the United States was that entrusting the leadership responsibilities to a group of twelve was sometimes problematic. Making decisions became difficult as consensus was not always readily achieved. As a result, and through prayer, God prompted us to choose four men from the gold group of twelve. These pastors are called the Faithful Four. These Faithful Four are the decision makers while we are in the United States on leave. These four help oversee the other groups. Eventually this group of four will provide full scope leadership in our region. We sense that our role has become that of facilitators. By facilitators, I mean that we will continue to bring pastors and lay people from the United States to help us disciple. Additionally, we will continue to facilitate with financial assistance when needed.

We have patiently waited for the moment when the Faithful Four would trust the Lord to embolden them with the necessary confidence. Thankfully, that day has happened. We were excited to receive an email from them, while we were in the United States, indicating they felt called to go to a prison about three hours away, via motorcycle, to minister and share the gospel. About a month later, six of the gold group pastors went and spent about five hours ministering and sharing the gospel. God moved and 200 prisoners were saved that day! These pastors began a prison ministry. This is just one more example of how God has moved through obedience.

Chapter 11: THE TEACHINGS

We started by teaching the basics of the Christian faith. After a couple of years, we knew we had to tackle the false teachings that were prevalent in the churches. Those false teachings are rooted in the culture, voodoo, and other religions mixing with voodoo. Many of these false teachings have been handed down, generation to generation. We take each topic and reveal truth from the Scriptures. God's Spirit works through the Scriptures in order to set the pastors free. Then, the pastors can go back to their churches and teach the truth to those in their churches. The list below includes a few of the false teachings:

- Ladies cannot teach or pray without a head covering.
- Ladies cannot attend church if they are wearing pants.
- If a lady is not married and has children, she cannot sing in the choir, be baptized, or take communion.
- You are not a pastor, even if called by God, if you are not recognized by the government or dressed properly.

- Pastors are obligated to others to physically feed and meet other physical needs.
- You must go to a certain mountain in Haiti to hear from God.
- A church is not a church if there aren't miracles.
- A funeral ceremony cannot be held in church for a person who is not a believer.
- It is considered good practice to get a woman pregnant before you marry her to make sure she can have children.
- Taking communion could cause you to die. Also, if you want to take communion, you must attend the business meeting on the Saturday before communion services. If you don't attend the business meeting, but still try to take communion, you will be subject to being embarrassed by others in a public setting.
- Salvation can only be attained at a certain age. However, there is no specific age that is referenced.
- Water baptism is only an option at a certain age. In order to be water baptized, a person must go through a course, take a test, and wear nice clothing. Only then can the person be baptized by the pastor.

Further compounding the spread of these false teachings is the fact that the illiteracy rate in Haiti is around 80%. Many people think the government is the sole oppressor of Haitians, but the church contributes to the oppression as well.

Chapter 12: LESSONS WE HAVE LEARNED

During the book study called Experiencing God by Henry Blackaby, which I mentioned earlier in the book, we learned valuable lessons. The seven points of the Experiencing God study are listed below, along with what we have experienced regarding each one of the points:

1. God is always at work around you. I saw Him working around me as I served Him at church and in the community. I also saw how He worked among Terry and I as we discipled the pastors and their wives in Haiti.

2. God pursues a continuing love relationship. Every time I thought God was done with me, He continued to pursue me and draw me back.

3. God invites you to get involved in His work. God prompted me to teach, beginning at There is Hope maternity home. Later we would go to Haiti.

4. God speaks through His Spirit through His church, circumstances, prayer etc. God spoke to me in the following specific ways. He spoke to me when I was in Clinton, Oklahoma during a church service. At that service, a lady called me

up front. She shared with me that God told her to tell me that I would soon be soon working with many women. I had already been praying about the pregnancy center and had specifically asked for confirmation.

5. <u>God's invitation will require faith and action.</u> I had to take a step of faith. That faith was combined with action in the form of going back to Clinton, Missouri. Then, back to Haiti again.

6. <u>You must make major adjustments to join Him</u>. I had to make major adjustments to move to a foreign country of which I knew nothing.

7. <u>You will come to know God by experience as you obey Him</u>. I have learned so much about His protection and faithfulness as I took small steps of faith. Those small steps of faith made it easier to take larger steps of faith in order to demonstrate my obedience to Him.

Another lesson we learned is that you can't out give God. We sold everything we owned in 2003 to go to Haiti full-time in 2004. We have built several houses in Haiti for families over the past 15 years. I had asked God for a place to call home in the United States. I wanted a home that my grandchildren could call "grandma's house." In 2017 God answered that prayer. Some dear friends gave us a house in Warsaw, Missouri. We are now staying in that home while on break in the states. The grandkids do come to visit and call it "grandma's house."

A practical lesson learned very quickly was that preparing and cooking food can be challenging, especially when you don't have running water, electricity, or a refrigerator. Having only one kerosene burner to cook and one kerosene lamp for light was challenging. We were so thankful after living in Haiti for a year when God blessed us with a refrigerator that used a propane tank. We then graduated to a two-burner propane cooktop stove along with a filter system to purify our water. This allowed us to not have to walk two miles for drinking water. We were also blessed with solar panels and four batteries which allowed us to have some lights at night. Eventually we would even become able to have a satellite dish for internet which allowed us to keep in touch with family, friends, and our church families. When was the last time you thanked God for what we think of as the simple things in life, such as a glass of ice, a refrigerator with a freezer to make the ice, being able to flip a switch for a light, or ways to communicate to keep in touch with family?

Before Terry and I went to Haiti, we learned a valuable lesson that would be used over and over in the years ahead. That lesson has been used in Haiti, one of the poorest countries in the world, where you have no choice but to totally rely on Him. However, we've also used the lesson learned everywhere he has led us. When the Lord prompted us to quit our jobs and go into full time ministry to serve Him, we learned to totally depend on Him, and He would take care of us. We learned that God is faithful to do what He says He will do, equip us for the task ahead, make a way when there seems to be no way, and to find great joy in serving God wherever He leads. His ways and His thoughts are much greater than ours.

Early on Terry shared with the pastors that they, their families, and the two of us would be attacked by satan for having faith in doing God's will. We saw that happen when the pastors were attacked by other pastors. We have had this happen as Haitian pastors have lied and tried to cause problems to get us out of Haiti. Satan doesn't like what we are doing. We have even had a pastor in the states condemn us because we aren't doing missions the way they have known or seen done.

When you are led by God's Spirit, the methods may not be like everyone else is doing it. We count it all joy, because we know if satan is attacking what he doesn't like, God is moving.

Through the years we learned that lack of transportation was an issue. In order to make remote discipleship more effective and efficient we purchased our first pickup truck. On our first trip up the mountain it got baptized. The journey takes us ten hours but is only a 150-mile trip. The roads are very rough. When we were about two hours out from our destination, we came upon an area called "little river." When we arrived at "little river" it was pouring down rain. The "little river" became a big river. We could not turn around because it would be getting dark soon. It is dangerous to be out on the roads after dark. Additionally, there might not have been any other better route. We prayed! Then Terry drove into the current of "little river." The truck was immediately covered with water. Suddenly, we were on the other side. There was no explanation for our safe passage other than God answering our prayers.

Chapter 13: THE WOMEN OF HAITI

Many women in Haiti have very low self-esteem. So, when I get a chance, I teach them who they are, as followers of Christ, from the Word of God. Below are a few of the Biblical principles that I share with the women:

- I am precious to God; Isaiah 43:4
- I am accepted by God; Ephesians 1:6
- I am a child of God; John 1:12
- I am chosen by God; 1 Peter 2:9-10
- I am justified (made righteous, just as if I had never sinned) by God; Romans 5:1
- I am sanctified (set apart for His service) before God; 1 Cor 6:11
- I am redeemed (bought with a price) by God; 1 Cor 6:20
- I am forgiven by God; 1 John 1:9
- I am a member of Christ's body; 1 Cor 12:27
- I am a saint, totally changed, and adopted by God; Eph 1:1 and 5
- I have been given everything I need by God; 2 Peter 1:3
- I have been given mercy (not given what I deserve); Hebrews 4:16

- I have been given grace (given what I don't deserve); James 4:6
- I have complete access to God; Ephesians 2:18 & 3:12
- I have the mind of Christ; 1 Corinthians 2:16

Additional areas the women are taken through, in order to renew their mind, are as follows:

- Believing God has a plan for their lives, that they are not an accident, and have been born for a purpose; Jeremiah 29:11
- Believing that outside circumstances do not control their lives; Psalm 7:3-5
- Believing God wants us to be blessed in every area of our lives; John 10:10
- Our priorities must line up with God's will and He must be first; Matt 6:33
- Be excellent in all you do; Psalm 8:1.

Chapter 14: A TYPICAL HAITIAN DAY

Very seldom are there two days alike. Here is a sample of daily life in Haiti.

- 4 a.m. Hear roosters crowing.
- 4-5 a.m. Wake up, get up, and have quiet time.
- 6 a.m. Light begins to come over the horizon.
- 6:15 a.m. Look out the window to see children picking the flowers in the yard and eating the stems. Or, the children are knocking almonds out of the trees and breaking them with a rock for a drop of food about the size of three grains of rice.
- 6:30 a.m. Go for a walk. See people out and about with hoes and machetes or carrying items to sell at a market somewhere. Begin to smell wood or charcoal cooking. See more children out scavenging for food. An elderly widow lady is looking for a dollar to buy a piece of bread. I give her a dollar. A young boy takes a goat somewhere to graze. Donkeys are loaded with wood, grass, or water going back home. Kids and youth are on their way to get water at the nearest spring. They will carry the water back on their heads. Sometimes the journey is as far as a mile away.

People greet me asking me where I am going because they don't understand why I would just be walking for my health. I pray with those that come by or are met on the road. Maintain solar lights and panels. Prepare drinking water. Prepare breakfast.

- Mid-morning: Walk to get food supplies needed for the day. Prepare the food purchased and then begin lunch.
- Afternoon: Get water from the cistern with buckets (because we have no running water.) Fix a shower bag with water to set in the sun to warm up for a late afternoon shower. Disciple and/or minister those who come. Go out with a pastor or someone else to do evangelism or other ministry.
- Late afternoon: Shower and then prepare something to eat for an evening snack. Retire to bed soon after dark. Hope to get some sleep without interruptions from roosters, donkeys, goats, or motorcycle horns.

On other days, if it is a rainy, no one goes anywhere. Schools have mud days instead of snow days. Tuesdays are our big market day to get grain and other nonperishables for the week.   On Sundays, Sunday school

(Bible study for all ages) starts anytime from 6 a.m. to 8 a.m. The church service starts one hour later. Services conclude after three or four hours of sitting on hard benches. On Sunday evenings the services usually last about two hours. During the week the church has an early morning prayer service around 4 or 5 a.m. as well as a prayer service one or two evenings a week.

Sometimes during the week those involved in voodoo have services which go well into the night; and sometimes all night. This makes for a rough night to sleep because they are very loud.

Facts about Haiti:

- The poorest country in the Western Hemisphere
- 10 million people inhabit Haiti
- Haiti's land space is about the size of Maryland
- Very little forest or cropland
- Average income is less than a dollar a day
- Illiteracy rate is 75% to 80%
- Life expectancy is 55 years

- The main food of rice is provided by outside resources, but they sustain themselves with small gardens
- In our area there is no electricity or plumbing
- Most survive by bartering
- When Haitians see white skin, they think you are very rich and that you should give them something
- Many Haitians believe they can be pregnant for two or more years
- Outside toilets
- Many are barefoot
- There is a strong spirit of poverty, oppression, and laziness
- Some believe they cannot learn
- Some believe they cannot help others
- Many suffer from the "I can't" syndrome, lack of faith, and complain
- Some sell their soul to voodoo for help.
- The spirit of religion is overwhelming (I define spirit of religion as man's laws added to God's laws, works instead of grace through faith, seeking things before God, going to another religion for healing and

help, legalism, going to another religion's leader for forgiveness, and worship of anything besides the one true God)

- Tin or thatch roofs on homes and churches are common along with, dirt or cement floors, and stick/mud or concrete block walls
- Church services and Sunday school last three to four hours
- Some walk great distances to find a church
- Most families do not have a Bible

Chapter 15: WHAT WE HAVE LEARNED

Through the years serving in Haiti, we have learned much about the people and culture. Here are some of the things we have discovered.

- Haitian people are relational and welcoming. They will gladly give up their food for others.
- Haitians quickly and positively interact with one another after an argument. Grudges are not held due to conflict or strife.
- Haitians spend most of their time outside; only going inside to sleep.
- The physical beauty of Haiti is breathtaking.
- Other missionaries don't care what church you belong to or come from. There is a spirit of teamwork among missionaries.
- Adjusting to not having running water is somewhat easy and a workout is obtained from carrying water. Many Haitians must walk a long way to find good clean water from a spring.
- In the province where we serve, we only have one restaurant. That restaurant does not have a menu. Additionally, you must pre-order a day or two ahead in addition to paying ahead of time. An

alternative is to take your chances, go to the restaurant, and have whatever they cooked for the day.

- The logistics of traveling anywhere in Haiti is difficult. As a result, travel only occurs to go get money or pick up someone coming to help or visit. People typically just stay in their geographic area. We always look forward to people coming to help as it is an answer to prayer.
- The government is corrupt, and it trickles down in society.
- The government oppresses the people.
- The false teachings and manmade rules in the church oppress the people.
- Haiti is very chaotic, especially the traffic.
- Customer service in most stores or businesses in the city is terrible.
- Judgment by skin color is common. We are perceived as being very rich and it can result in paying higher prices for products or services. Additionally, people believe we have something to give away and they expect us to do so.
- It is difficult and painful to establish trusting relationships. It is hard to get the truth of a matter as the spirit of confusion is strong and active. We

are very thankful that we now have some trusting relationships which helps offset this issue.

- Many government employees, police officers, and teachers don't get paid for months or years, even though there is money to pay them.
- Living among the impoverished can be emotionally exhausting, which causes the need to set up boundaries. Many emotions are experienced all at the same time and all five senses are used simultaneously.
- There is cultural acceptance of physical punishment out in the open.
- There is a lack of a father's presence in many families.
- There is sometimes a lack of affection toward babies and children. This can be caused due to constantly having to work to find or prepare food as well as doing laundry by hand.
- Many orphanage systems are very corrupt. What is more surprising is how many people are blind to this corruption.
- The feeling of being so far away from people back home. This is a common feeling among missionaries.

- Medical and educational systems are very poor and inferior.
- Most Haitians do not have electricity. A few may have a kerosene lamp. Sometimes kerosene lamps have caused thatch roof houses to burn.
- In the province where we serve, Haitians walk everywhere, unless they have money for a motorcycle.
- It is like two different worlds between the cities and the provinces.
- Many do not know their date of birth.
- Many do not have any form of identification.
- Getting anything done in Haiti requires much time and energy. It's difficult to explain to people back home because they live in a society where service is generally fast and quick.

Chapter 16: THE CALL TO ARMS

Although we are saved by faith in Christ alone, our obedience to God's commands validates our confession. The Christian life begins when we believe and turn our lives over to Jesus Christ. At that moment we become a new creation, sealed by God's Spirit. Then, we become part of the Master's plan to go and tell others. To grow as disciples, we must be obedient to the calling to know Him intimately and to make Him known to others at all costs. (Luke 9:23)

Christ commands us to go and make disciples. Our responsibility is to testify to the lost by word and deed. God's Spirit convicts and then He does the saving. Water baptism is an outward expression of an internal supernatural change that has taken place in one's life by turning toward God (repentance) and faith in Jesus, His Son. Water baptism identifies us with Christ in His death, burial, and resurrection.

Life in Christ demands a total transformation of our lives. We need God's help in the Christian walk every day. His ways should be the basis by which we live all aspects of life. Christ should be at the center of all we do. We should be actively learning and imparting that knowledge to others. Every time you start to go back to the old self or addictions to sin, you should hear something from God's Spirit like, "No, that is not how we act or talk in this family." If you are truly a child of God, you can't continue in a lifestyle of sin and not be miserable as conviction is felt from God's Spirit.

If you do not know Jesus as Savior, that transition can be easily made. Salvation is a free gift. However, once you receive that free gift, there is a cost. We must all accept, by faith, Christ's death on the cross. His shed blood is the payment for your sins. That payment allows you to trust Him to be your Savior.

Being part of a Bible believing New Testament church is important. I encourage you to surrender all and be willing to go and do whatever God is leading you to do. God desires to increase your territory.

Spread the message of Jesus, called evangelizing, as well as teach and disciple others in the ways of God. Spend time with God in prayer and study His Word, the Bible. Ask God to break your heart for what breaks His.

When the roll is called up yonder, I'll be there, will you?

If you aren't sure about where you will spend eternity, please spend some time reading, studying, and reflecting on the rest of the material in this chapter. The rest of this chapter is used with permission from our friend, Alan Balmer, and is from his book the *40 Day Lent Vocabulary Devotional* which is found on Amazon at the following link.

http://amzn.com/B01MYEKAP1

That book, and his *100 Day Vocabulary Word Devotional* will help you as you continue on in the discipleship process.

http://amzn.com/B01NARVGW3

Word for the Day:
commutation [kom-y*uh*-**tey**-sh*uh* n] noun
1.the act of substituting one thing for another; substitution; exchange.
2. the changing of a prison sentence or other penalty to another less severe.
3. the act of commuting, as to and from a place of work.
4. the substitution of one kind of payment for another.
5. *Electricity.* the act or process of commutating.
6. Also called commutation test. *Linguistics.* the technique, especially in phonological analysis, of substituting one linguistic item for another while keeping the surrounding elements constant, used as a means of determining the constituent units in a sequence and their contrasts with other units.

commutation. Dictionary.com. Dictionary.com Unabridged. Random House, Inc. http://www.dictionary.com/browse/commutation (accessed: January 7, 2017).

The concept of this word includes something being substituted, exchanged or traded.

Scripture for the Day:
Isaiah 53:5-6 (NASB)
5 But He was pierced through for our transgressions, He was crushed for our iniquities; the chastening for our well-being fell upon Him, and by His scourging we are healed. 6 All of us like sheep have gone astray, each of us has turned to his own way; but the LORD has caused the iniquity of us all to fall on Him.

Devotion for the Day:

As you begin this 40-day journey, which will help you reflect on what Jesus Christ did for you, the first of the 40 days of devotionals is written to ensure that you have a foundational basis for what Jesus Christ accomplished for you and all humanity. The following outline will give you some perspective on realizing THE spiritual problem, understanding the results stemming from it, how to resolve it, and the role of Jesus in assisting us with it.

REALIZING THE PROBLEM

1 Corinthians 6:9a (NASB95) says, "Or do you not know that the unrighteous will not inherit the kingdom of God?" The Bible gives us a clear understanding of what unrighteousness is and defines it as sin. **Galatians 5:19-21 (NASB95)** gives us additional Biblical insight into sin as follows;

19 "Now the deeds of the flesh are evident, which are: immorality, impurity, sensuality, 20 idolatry, sorcery, enmities, strife, jealousy, outbursts of anger, disputes, dissensions, factions, 21 envying, drunkenness, carousing, and things like these, of which I forewarn you, just as I have forewarned you, that those who practice such things will not inherit the Kingdom of God."

You can also review the following passages of Scripture that will give you additional insight (Ephesians 5:3-5, Matthew 15:19, Exodus 20:1-17). It becomes clear that the Bible has a negative view of SIN; it is wrong. SIN is the

PROBLEM. Let's now come to an understanding of the results of SIN.

RESULTS OF THE PROBLEM

First of all, let's establish the reach of sin and see who it impacts. **Romans 3:23 (NASB)** says, "For all have sinned and fall short of the glory of God." and **1 John 1:10 (NASB)** says, "If we say that we have not sinned, we make Him a liar and His word is not in us." So, to whom does this problem pertain? It pertains to everyone (that includes me and you reading this!). Now that we understand the PROBLEM pertains to me, you and all humanity, let's look at the consequences of sin.

Romans 6:23a (NASB), "For the wages of sin is death."

Matthew 5:29-30 (NASB), 29 "If your right eye makes you stumble, tear it out and throw it from you; for it is better for you to lose one of the parts of your body, than for your whole body to be thrown into hell. 30 If your right hand makes you stumble, cut it off and throw it from you; for it is better for you to lose one of the parts of your body, than for your whole body to go into hell."

Revelation 20:12-15 (NASB), "12 And I saw the dead, the great and the small, standing before the throne, and books were opened; and another book was opened, which is *the book* of life; and the dead were judged from the things which were written in the books, according to their deeds. 13 And the sea gave up the dead which were in it,

and death and Hades gave up the dead which were in them; and they were judged, every one *of them* according to their deeds. 14 Then death and Hades were thrown into the lake of fire. This is the second death, the lake of fire.
15 And if anyone's name was not found written in the book of life, he was thrown into the lake of fire."

Here we see the problem with SIN is that it results in spiritual death, and ultimately an eternity in hell. But there is good news; there is a way to resolve this problem. Let's see how the resolution occurs.

RESOLVING THE PROBLEM

Now that we REALIZE the RESULTS of the PROBLEM, let's come to an understanding of how we RESOLVE the PROBLEM by examining a few passages of Scripture.

Romans 6:23 (NASB), "For the wages of sin is death, but the free gift of God is eternal life in Christ Jesus our Lord."

Ephesians 2:8-9 (NASB), 8 "For by grace you have been saved through faith; and that not of yourselves, *it is* the gift of God; 9 not as a result of works, so that no one may boast."

2 Corinthians 7:10 (NASB), "For the sorrow that is according to *the will of* God produces a repentance without regret, *leading* to salvation, but the sorrow of the world produces death."

Other verses to review on your own: 1 Peter 3:18, Matthew 4:17, Philippians 2:10-11.

In spite of the severe consequences of sin, Jesus performed an act of substitution on our behalf when he went willingly to the cross in order to be crucified. In that one act, He bore the penalty of our sin and exchanged His life for our life. What should have been a verdict of guilty for you, me, and all humanity was wiped clean by this unreal act of His love that He performed for our benefit. In order for you to avoid an eternity of judgment in hell, you must accept the gift that Jesus performed on the cross by trusting, relying on, and believing in Him. Please take a moment of self-reflection by reading and answering the following questions.

1. Are you a sinner?
2. Do you believe that your sin has caused you the ultimate consequence of spiritual death, which results in an eternity in hell?
3. Do you want forgiveness for your sins? Do you want to change your destiny from hell to heaven?
4. Do you believe Jesus died on the cross for you, rose again, and that He is the only way to heaven?
5. Are you willing to surrender your life to Jesus Christ; meaning that you will be obedient to follow His will, stop sinning, and work for the Kingdom of God?
6. If you believe and agree with the above, you are ready to pray as follows.
    1. Pray to invite Jesus into your life and your heart.

2. Pray to ask Jesus for forgiveness for your sins (to be your Savior).
3. Pray to ask Jesus for help to stop sinning.
4. Pray to make a commitment to follow Jesus (to let Him be your Lord).
5. Pray to make a commitment to work for the Kingdom of God instead of the kingdom of the devil.

Bottom Line for the Day:

I hope that after reading the devotion for the day that one of two things happened; either you confirmed that you have already trusted and believed in Jesus for eternity, or you recognized that your eternal destiny was not what you would like for it to be and then you prayed to receive Jesus Christ as your Lord and Savior. The act of accepting the commutation (substitution, exchange or trade) that Jesus Christ performed on the cross is the best decision you could ever make. As a final application today please read the lyrics listed below which are from the Chris Tomlin song "Jesus Messiah". This song incorporates the verse 2 Corinthians 5:21 which says,

"He made Him who knew no sin *to be* sin on our behalf, so that we might become the righteousness of God in Him." (NASB).

Lastly, consider listening to the song Jesus Messiah by Chris Tomlin at the completion of this devotion in order to have one final moment of reflection on what Jesus did for you.

He became sin, who knew no sin
That we might become His righteousness
He humbled Himself and carried the cross

Love so amazing, love so amazing

Jesus Messiah, name above all names
Blessed Redeemer, Emmanuel
The rescue for sinners, the ransom from Heaven
Jesus Messiah, Lord of all

Chapter 17: A MISSIONARY

A missionary is someone who goes out with intent to live each day by serving and following Jesus through evangelizing and discipling as in Matthew 28:18-20.

*(NKJV) **18** And Jesus came and spoke to them, saying, "All authority has been given to Me in heaven and on earth. **19** Go therefore and make disciples of all the nations, baptizing them in the name of the Father and of the Son and of the Holy Spirit, **20** teaching them to observe all things that I have commanded you; and lo, I am with you always, even to the end of the age." Amen.*

Sometimes we are called to a specific place and time to do a specific work. Anyone can be a missionary wherever they are, but there must have a heart for missions. I define having a missionary's heart with the following bullet points.

- Knowing God
- Surrendering all to God
- Following Christ whatever the cost
- Being outwardly focused rather than inwardly focused

- Having Christ as the center of your life
- Exhibiting compassion, love, mercy, and forgiveness for others, just as with the example of Jesus

Maybe God is prompting you to leave all for Him. Maybe He is calling you to go to a specific place. You are never too old or too young. I want you to know, however, that it can be a difficult journey. Sometimes you may experience grief, disappointment, and be taken advantage of. Jesus never promised a rose garden, meaning it won't always be easy. There will be sacrifices to make. When we follow Him with our whole heart and become a true follower, Jesus said persecution would follow. We may not have a place to lay our heads for rest. And, those in your own household will come against you. Being away from friends and family is hard, and sometimes results in a feeling of desertion. Once new friends are gained on the mission field, it is difficult to leave them and return to the states. But there is also no greater joy than serving our Lord and seeing those you serve and work with come to Christ and then seeing them disciple others. In Hebrews 13:5 He promises He will never leave you nor forsake you. In Matthew 28:20 He promises He will be with you always. He is faithful to get us through the valleys so we can experience the mountain tops.

Chapter 18: 20 YEARS AND COUNTING

Serving Christ in Haiti for the past 20 years has increased my faith and helped me to understand so much more about poverty, how the church can oppress people, and how God's love, grace and mercy can free anyone from any problem. I have seen God's people trust Him fully as they have no other source of hope.

I don't know what God has in store for the next 20 years, but I do desire to continue going and serving wherever He leads. I haven't seen anything in the Bible about retirement from serving Him. I know that He will not lead me astray and that He will be with me as he guides every step. He may not take me out of the valley, but He will walk by my side through that valley. I may not reach the goal He has set before me when I think I should, but He will get me there in His perfect timing. He continues to be my strength when I am weak.

I have learned that I should not try to change the culture. Rather, I show those who I am discipling from God's Word where the culture or traditions are opposed to the Word of God. Then we encourage them to trust God for help in making the necessary changes.

Until God calls me home or Jesus returns, I desire to spend my time wisely and I hope you will as well. Serve Him. Be ready for His return. Ultimately, I want to hear Him say, "Well done, My good and faithful servant." Time and devotion are the most valuable assets you can give to someone. Not all opportunities are from God. Satan will try to lead you astray because he doesn't like it when we are being obedient to, and following God. Take control of your schedule and live a life that matters, serving Christ however He leads. God, through His Spirit, will help you remove the things that are holding you back from doing what is most needed in this season of your life. Your life can be a legacy that your children and grandchildren will know and remember as they watch, and hopefully follow your example. Our choices, character, love, and obedience will live on long after we are gone from this world. Our walk with God should be a positive model to those who are watching and will leave a mark on the hearts and lives of all who love us.

Over the past 20 years, and even before that, I have realized that I am set apart because I am a child of God. Just like Queen Esther in the Old Testament, He sets us apart to be obedient to that which He calls us. Sometimes it comes at a great cost. Some will admire you for your dedication. Some may even try to put you on a pedestal. Some will want you to fail. And, some will not understand. I know from experience that I am not perfect, and neither will you be perfect. However, our mistakes can tutor us to becoming wiser. Let Him set you apart to be a witness to the world wherever He leads you.

What have you been doing the past 20 years? It is never too late to start focusing on missions. Matthew 28:18-20 says to "Go." It doesn't say unless you have young children, a job, too busy, too old, too young, not equipped, too shy, etc. I want to encourage you and your family to get involved in missions. You are never too old, and your children or grandchildren are never too young. Start in your neighborhood, your city, your state, then beyond. Matthew 28:18-20 also says to "make disciples." Once we share the gospel, and someone chooses to follow Jesus, it is our responsibility to disciple them so they can do the same with others that they lead to Him.

A simple way to start is in your neighborhood. Take a loaf of bread with a written scripture on it to your neighbor. Be a blessing. Ask how you can pray for your neighbor. Another way to start is to simply take a light bulb or bottled water and do the same as with the loaf of bread. If your town or city has a nursing home or homeless shelter, go and serve. Take your children and let them read a Bible verse or sing a song. Be an example to others. If there is not a designated person in your church to lead missions; volunteer to take that position. Then, lead others to go with you to an area to do missions where you can involve your whole family. Missions will grow your faith as well as your family's faith. Missions has strengthened our family and I know it can do the same for yours. Teaching your children and grandchildren God's Word and being an example to them by doing and taking them on mission trips is the greatest thing you can do for them, or any others you can disciple.

Earlier in this chapter I mentioned that obedience and faithfulness can have an impact on the lives of children and grandchildren. I defined that impact as legacy. As we conclude this chapter, please find below the words of our children, regarding their perspective, as it pertains to our life of service and to missions.

Myra (oldest)

I recall in 2015 our church talking about the two billion people and 16,000 people groups who have never heard the gospel. As Christians we are called to spread the good news. It has been hard over the years with my parents, my children's grandparents, living in Haiti. I wish I could see them more and sometimes ask, "Why them?" I was reminded during that 2015 day how the need is great, and the workers are few. I am thankful for their sacrifice, obedience, and example to my children. So, whatever God calls us to do...pray, send, or go...we need to be ready and willing.

Little did I know, a few months later, our family would be asked to go to China for my husband's work assignment. I felt God laying this on my heart, asking me if I was willing to go. My mom was there to talk me through it and encourage me to trust God's plan. After going to China, we were able to see God work in and through our family in so many ways, to experience a different people group, and develop our own stories of God's faithfulness.

Through our experience, my children have learned a new appreciation for what their grandparents do. They love to hear their grandparents' many stories of God's faithfulness in Haiti. One night, as I was putting my 13-year-old to bed, Madyson recalled one of grandma's stories of God speaking to her. She looked at me and said, "I hope God will speak to me like that someday. It would be so cool and much easier to know what to do!" Megan and Miranda have also enjoyed the stories. They always ask to hear the "cookie story" (which was told in a previous chapter.) They have enjoyed many Skype calls which would sometimes include meeting many adults and children, as well as the occasional baby goat or chicken, who passed by while they were talking via Skype on the computer.

Mackenzie has always had a special bond with her grandparents. When they are in Haiti, she loves playing Show and Tell with her toys, and teatime on Skype. No matter how long they are apart, when reunited it seems as if no time has passed. Even from a very young age Mackenzie was inseparable from Grandma Carolyn.

John

This is the perspective of the son of parents who became missionaries in the later part of their lives. I was still in college when my parents sold everything and moved to Haiti as missionaries. I became friends with other students under similar circumstances, mainly missionary kids (or MK's as they called themselves.) Those students attended college in the US, while their parents were scattered across the globe spreading the gospel. I was in normal communication with Mom and remember not being overly surprised, just worried. Mom had been on a few mission trips to Haiti and seemed to find joy in the experience. At the time, I knew little of the country outside of abject poverty and consistent political unrest. My main concerns were directed towards Mom's safety. Shortly after graduating from college, I decided to travel and visit Mom in Haiti. I also included a trip to Brazil with a friend from college. The trip to Brazil was a good intermediate destination before traveling to Haiti. The trip to Haiti would be like jumping into the deep end by comparison.

I traveled to Haiti with a mission team who was planning to build a church. Once we got off the plane, all eyes were on us as the street vendors saw us as rich tourists. Outside the airport there was an old deuce-and-a-half military-style cargo truck waiting. This truck ride would be the most significant event of the trip for me. The discomfort of the truck ride was indescribable. I recall squatting like a baseball catcher for the last few hours of the trip. Mom got quite a laugh for the following three or four days as I ate my meals standing up. The chairs they had at the table were not padded, and it hurt too much to sit on them.

After helping the mission group build the church, I stayed with my parents for a couple of months at the orphanage they led. Spending time where my parents lived was a blessing in more than one way. I was able to meet some of the people in the surrounding area. They saw my parents as a lifeline of support for those in need as well as a valuable asset to the community. My parents' safety was just as important to the community as it was to me. After spending time there, my concern for mom's safety was greatly minimized.

Mom and Terry have lived in Haiti since before my children were born and have not always been available for help or advice. But they have still played a major role in raising and caring for my children by spending quality time with them when they are back in the states. I think there is a natural bond between grandparents and grandkids, as well as a strong desire for grandparents to show love to their grandkids. Our children are old enough to miss their grandparents. The oldest asks when "GG" and "Papa" will come back, and why they must go to Haiti. I know that Mom and Terry miss their family and we miss them. This is the greatest cost of being a missionary. Being a veteran from the Army, from what I can tell, mission work is like being in the military. You are in a place you have been called to serve, while those you love most carry on with their lives thousands of miles away. I do look forward to the day when my parents can retire from the mission field and spend more time with their grandkids. I hope it is when God is able to replace them with the next generation of missionaries.

Stefany

As the youngest daughter of Terry and Carolyn, I have loved seeing their dedication to their ministry. Their selflessness and love for the needy has been a huge influence in my life. It is sometimes tough to not have them around for the big moments back in the states, especially now that I have a daughter of my own, but I know how important it is that they are passing on the love of Christ in a country like Haiti.

Chapter 19: THE WHY AND HOW

Many times, over the years I have asked God, "Why me Lord?" Each time He has answered, "Because you were and still are willing to follow Me no matter the cost." Many times, my heart was willing, but the flesh was weak. However, during those weak moments I have said, "There is no greater joy than being obedient to His voice. I will go and serve where He leads and stay in the center of His will."

Through the years, many have asked why we do what we do and then inquire how it is accomplished. Specifically, people ask how we could sell everything, live in the poorest country in the world, have no running water or electricity, and, most of all, live by faith. One day while at a beach with other missionaries who received a salary from their organization, a young lady told me, "I wish I could live by faith like you do, for God to provide everything."

The following is my heart song:

Oh how I love Jesus
Oh how I love Jesus
Oh how I love Jesus
Because HE FIRST LOVED ME

When I read and study the scriptures about what Jesus did for me, it is sufficient to answer the WHY portion of the question. Jesus was flogged under the command of Pilate. He was taken away and stripped. He was made to kneel before a three-foot pillar with iron rings embedded in each side. Guards tied His wrists with a rope. A whip was used for the punishment. That whip had a wooden handle with nine leather cords and included tips of bone, small links of metal chain and other sharp objects. The executioner took the whip, spread his feet for traction, and stood six feet behind Jesus. With a flick of his wrist, the guard struck Jesus with the whip in the area of His ribs and shoulders. Then the guard jerked back the leather, tearing off pieces of flesh and spattering blood on the floor. By the time the flogging was over His skin was eaten away. I can't imagine the PAIN!

Jesus was then taken to a holding area with harsh, military men. As they cut the ropes from His wrists, He must have fallen from the pain and weakness due to blood loss. They were cruel and heartless during this harassment. They tore His blood-soaked clothing from His body, had Him stand naked, alone, and with no one to defend Him. Throughout all of this, He did not open His mouth.

They commanded Jesus to sit while a soldier balled his hand into a fist and hit Him. Another soldier hit Him. And yet, another soldier took a strand of thorns and wove it into a wreath to place it on the head of Jesus as a crown. That soldier pushed the crown thorns into Jesus' scalp. Another soldier spat on Jesus. All of this He endured for me and YOU!

By now Jesus had suffered loss of sleep, loss of blood, and loss of his friends. The soldiers gave Him a vertical beam to carry to Golgotha, the place of the skull, where they would nail Him to that very beam. That beam would be used along with another beam to make a cross. The cross was the cruelest punishment. Blood oozing from His body, exhausted, and sweating, He was wrestled to the ground. They placed Him on the cross beams and with an iron mallet nailed his hands/wrists and feet to the cross. The weight of His body would tear the skin and muscles from His arms. With the strength Jesus had, He said, "Father, forgive them, they know not what they do."

Later, the soldiers offered Jesus sour wine to quench His thirst. Then, they would sponge His wounds with something like alcohol while laughing because they knew it stung and burned. They told Him that if He was truly the Christ, He should save himself. He could have saved himself or He could have saved us; but He couldn't do both. Despite how much pain He experienced, how tired He was, how weak, and how alone; Jesus had the strength to choose us! He hung on that cross several hours then said, "It is finished." But the story doesn't end there. The soldiers put Jesus in a tomb and satan thought Jesus was dead for good. But, NO, on the third day HE AROSE!! He is now preparing a place for those who put their faith and trust in Him and follow Him in obedience.

He chose you and me to be His before the foundation of the earth was created. You are royalty, even though it is something you may not realize. He will wait for you until you are ready to start personally living out the amazing plan which He has set forth for you. He knows you don't know where to begin or how to become that which He has called you. Just let Him teach you day by day. Start by recognizing who He is as the King of kings and Lord of lords. Jesus is the Lover of your soul. When you meet with Jesus every day, He will show you how to let go of the things in your life that are holding you back from receiving the blessings which He wants to give. Remember, He has chosen you, and given you a choice to represent Him to the world. If you are willing, He is there to give you all you need to complete your calling. That calling is found below in John 15:16.

> **(NKJV) 16** *You did not choose Me, but I chose you and appointed you that you should go and bear fruit, and that your fruit should remain, that whatever you ask the Father in My name He may give you.*

Our love for Christ, what He did for us on the Cross, and the love He has put in our hearts for the lost Haitian people keep us involved in the Haitian mission field. God uses your love for us, your encouragement, your prayers, and your financial giving to make it possible for us to be devoted to the people of Haiti. Your support allows us to minister and disciple pastors so they can be equipped to evangelize, disciple, and be effective at shepherding the Haitian people into truth.

Chapter 20: CONCLUSION

My prayer for you, as you have read in the preceding chapter regarding how Jesus died and rose again for everyone, is that you now fully understand why we do what we do for the Haitian people. We are willing to go anywhere else God says go, no matter the cost. I also trust that this book will encourage you to follow Jesus faithfully wherever He may lead you.

While we were still sinners, Christ died for me and you!

Do you have your passport ready? There is an old Christian song, which has the lyrics repeated several times, which state the following:

"Where He leads me, I will follow"

How can you be obedient to follow Him anywhere if you are restricted to your country of residence through the lack of a passport?

At this point you have either skipped to the last page or you have completed reading this book. Either way, my prayer for you is the following:

1. That you have chosen Christ to be your Lord and Savior, putting your total trust in Him as you follow His Word in obedience; no matter the cost.
2. That you have or will follow Christ in obedience through water baptism.
3. That you will serve in a church who teaches and follows His Word.
4. That you will be intentional to go on mission trips wherever He leads, for the purpose of making disciples.
5. Finally, my prayer for you is that after reading this book, if you are hurting or feel abandoned, that you won't feel that way any longer. God will bring you out of whatever despair you are in if you will allow Him to. If, on the other hand, your life is going great, but you feel something is missing, God will fill that emptiness. If you need to reach out to someone, I encourage you to find someone you can trust to provide help. Or, feel free to contact me through the ways listed in the beginning of this book.

Maybe you are already one of the people who are following God in full devotion to Him no matter the cost. If so, keep up the good work, don't get discouraged, and be on guard and ready for any fiery darts satan may send your way. By putting on the full armor of God as listed in Ephesians 6, satan is overcome.

Made in the
USA
Columbia, SC